SUMMARY OF

THE MAN WHO SOLVED THE MARKET:

How Jim Simons Launched the Quant Revolution

By
Gregory Zuckerman

CTPrint

ISBN: 9781671788909

**CTPrint
Copyright (c) 2019**

All rights reserved. No part of this publication may be reproduced, distributed, or transmitted in any form or by any means, including photocopying, recording, or other electronic or mechanical methods, without the prior written permission of the publisher, except in the case of brief quotations embodied in critical reviews and certain other non commercial uses permitted by copywrite Law.

DISCLAIMER
This is a summary and meant to be a great companionship to the original book or to simply help you get the gist of the original book.

Table of Content

SYNOPSIS 5

ABOUT THE AUTHOR 6

INTRODUCTION 7

JIM SIMONS WAS OBSESSED WITH MATH FROM A VERY EARLY AGE. 9

SOON AFTER HIS STUDIES, SIMONS ENTERED ACADEMIA, BUT qUIT SUDDENLY TO CRACK SOVIET CODES FOR AN INTELLIGENCE AGENCY. 12

SIMONS HAD ENORMOUS SUCCESS IN GEOMETRY AND DEVELOPED A NEW STOCK-TRADING SYSTEM. 16

AFTER A SECOND STINT IN ACADEMIA, SIMONS FOUNDED THE HEDGE FUND MANAGEMENT FIRM, MONEMETRICS. 20

SIMONS NAMED HIS MONEMETRICS FUND AFTER A CHARACTER IN A JOSEPH CONRAD NOVEL – AND THIS WAS REVEALING 24

SIMONS INTRODUCED COMPUTERS INTO THE WORLD OF INVESTMENT WITH GREAT SUCCESS. 27

SIMONS' CAREER BROUGHT HIM INTO THE AMBIT OF A BRILLIANT MAN WHO WOULD GO ON TO COURT GREAT CONTROVERSY. 31

WHEN ALL IS SAID AND DONE, JIM SIMONS' CV IS AN ASTONISHING DOCUMENT. 35

FINAL SUMMARY..39
ABOUT CTPRINT 40

SYNOPSIS:

The Man Who Solved the Market (2019) traces the life of enigmatic hedge fund manager and mathematician Jim Simons. It chronicles his early life as a brilliant geometer who won awards for his math, to his work breaking Soviet codes, all the way through to his success with his hedge fund management firm Renaissance Technologies. Far more than just another investor, Simons changed the world with his math and methods.

ABOUT THE AUTHOR:

Gregory Zuckerman Is a Special Writer at The Wall Street Journal. He's a three-time winner of the Gerald Loeb award, which is the highest honor in business journalism. As well as The Man Who Solved The Market, he is the author of The Frackers and The Greatest Trade Ever.

Disclaimer: This book is not meant to replace the original book but to serve as a companion to it.

INTRODUCTION.

Delve into the life of an enigmatic hedge fund manager and mathematician.

Jim Simons likes to watch for patterns in the financial markets. He sees them as beautiful, mysterious forms, like great shoals of fish or the nebulae in the night sky. He knows that behind these patterns – like everything else in the universe – is mathematics. And by using mathematics, he knows that he can predict changes in these patterns. And by doing that, he can make money – and lots of it.

Jim Simons is the most successful investor in modern history. His hedge fund firm, Renaissance Technologies, is discussed in reverent tones in the business world – it sets the gold standard globally, with financial analysts trying to understand its secretive, ground-breaking methods.

But Jim Simons is much more than a Wall Street money man: an award-winning geometer, code-breaker, and philanthropist, he's had a career that should span several lifetimes. To sample a little of his extraordinary life, start at these blinks.

You'll find out

How Simons grasped Zeno's paradox at the age of four;
Why he named his hedge fund after a Joseph Conrad novel; and
What he didn't wear when lecturing on mathematics.

JIM SIMONS WAS OBSESSED WITH MATH FROM A VERY EARLY AGE.

Jim Simons loved numbers from the moment he understood what they were.

Born in 1938 to a middle-class American Jewish family in Brookline, Massachusetts, Jim was the only child of Matthew and Marcia Simons.

Like many people with an unusual talent for numbers, he began to show an interest in them very early. He learned to solve complex problems at the age of three. One day, his parents found him dividing numbers by two, all the way from 1024 downwards. For a toddler, this was an astonishing feat.

Another time, when out on a family drive, four-year-old Jim was baffled when his father had to stop to fill the car up with gas. Jim couldn't work out why this was necessary, as he figured that the tank wouldn't ever run out. He reasoned that if they used up half of what was in the tank, there would be another half remaining; then they could use half of that remaining half, leaving another, smaller half to be used, and so on.

Without knowing it, the four-year-old had started on a classic mathematical problem – one of the problems the Greek philosopher Zeno had addressed in his group of paradoxes. If you always have to travel half the remaining distance before reaching your destination, no matter how small, how can you ever reach your destination?

After school, he was encouraged to go into medicine by the family doctor, who thought it was a good job for "a bright Jewish boy." Of course, Jim had other ideas.

He enrolled at MIT and studied for a bachelor's degree in mathematics. After struggling initially and failing a few tests, he took time out one summer to really nail the more complex theorems. After that period, he began to blossom. He loved how complex formulae seemed to join up with other formulae across mathematics, seeming to hint at a universal system. He wondered if he was looking at a kind of code that could explain the world's mystery. He was often seen around campus lying on his back, eyes closed, contemplating an equation.

One time he saw two of his professors, renowned mathematicians, Warren Ambrose and Isadore Singer, deep in discussion at midnight in a local café. At that moment, he decided that this was the kind of life he wanted: cigarettes, coffee, and mathematics at all hours.

SOON AFTER HIS STUDIES, SIMONS ENTERED ACADEMIA, BUT qUIT SUDDENLY TO CRACK SOVIET CODES FOR AN INTELLIGENCE AGENCY.

After glittering academic achievements at MIT and Berkeley, Simons looked for a lecturing post.

At Berkeley, he'd completed his PhD in two years. It dealt with the geometry of multidimensional curved spaces. Its brilliance was enough to secure a teaching job at Harvard University.

He was a popular professor there, with an informal, enthusiastic style that matched his casual dress (so casual, in fact, that he sometimes didn't bother wearing socks). He approached teaching with a beginner's freshness, admitting, in certain cases, that he knew little more than his students about particularly complex bits of algebra.

However, at a certain point, he tired of teaching. His life had begun to follow a predictable pattern, with a cycle of lectures and polite academic socializing, and he was terminally bored. He needed another challenge.

So, before long, in 1964, Simons left Harvard to work for an intelligence group helping to fight the Cold War. This was the Institute for Defence Analysis, an elite research organization that hired mathematicians to help crack Soviet codes.

At the time, the IDA was struggling. They hadn't actually cracked Soviet codes on a regular basis for over a decade. Because of this lack of success, they decided to employ people like Simons, without code-breaking experience, for their pure brainpower. This meant that the place teemed with people like Simons: lovers of obscure theorems and long arguments about math. The IDA motto was "bad ideas is good, good ideas is terrific, no ideas is bad." It was here that Simons learned how to develop mathematical models to interpret patterns in seemingly meaningless data. And it was here that Simons developed an ultrafast code-breaking algorithm.

Shortly after Simons' innovation, intelligence experts in Washington discovered that a coded message with an incorrect setting had been sent by the Soviets. Simons and his colleagues leaped on this glitch and used their code-breaking model to better understand and exploit the enemy's internal messaging system. This led to Simons becoming something of a star at IDA and in the code-breaking community generally.

However, even this success wasn't enough for Jim's restless mind. He yearned for more mathematical challenges, more cryptic codes to unlock.

SIMONS HAD ENORMOUS SUCCESS IN GEOMETRY AND DEVELOPED A NEW STOCK-TRADING SYSTEM.

While trying to crack codes at IDA, employees had a great deal of time on their hands. Simons used his productively – to research and to ponder the world of global finance.

Meanwhile, while still at IDA, his research into geometry began to pay dividends. He focussed on theoretical questions, rather than those with immediate practical utility. This was what might be called pure math, absorbing him for days in abstract reflection. His area of research was on something called "minimal varieties" – a highly complex subject that dealt with the question of surface area.

A classic case concerns the surface formed by a soap film stretched across a wire frame that has been dipped in a soapy solution. The soap film has the smallest possible surface area compared with any other type of surface stretched between the same wire frame. Because such a surface is so smooth, no matter how complicated or twisted the wire frame, every point on this "minimal area" looks the same. Simons wanted to know if the same would be true of minimal surfaces in higher dimensions, rather than simply the two-dimensional wire frame.

In 1968, he published his research in "Minimal Varieties in Riemannian Manifolds," which helped establish him as one of the world's preeminent geometers.

But this wasn't enough to keep Simons occupied. Eager to earn more money, he began thinking about ways to use his talent for numbers to measure the stock market.

Rather than the tried-and-tested investment methods, which took into account earnings and corporate news, Simons began to approach the market in the same way that he looked at math: as an abstract intellectual system. He developed a model that simply considered "moves" in the stocks themselves, rather than looking at the outside context.

He posited that the market had eight underlying "states", such as "high variance," when stocks moved erratically, or "good," when they rose generally, for example. It was a system that wasn't interested in "why" the market entered certain states, but simply observed the different states and allowed investors to make bets accordingly.

Though his work was crude compared with today's market thinking, he was something of a trailblazer in his time. Eventually, predictive theory across different fields would resemble his method.

AFTER A SECOND STINT IN ACADEMIA, SIMONS FOUNDED THE HEDGE FUND MANAGEMENT FIRM, MONEMETRICS.

In 1968, after revealing to colleagues that he opposed the Vietnam War, Jim was fired from his code-breaking role at IDA.

Stunned, he looked for another job and soon returned to academia. He was appointed chairman of the math department at Stony Brook University, New York. But still, the world beyond the lecture hall beckoned. To the bafflement of many of his academic colleagues, at the age of forty, he left and founded Monemetrics, a hedge fund management firm. He wanted to find the hidden pattern in the markets. Also, he had to admit to himself, he wanted to be very rich. Unlike his academic colleagues, he was attracted to money.

His first move was to invite an old friend from IDA, Leonard Baum, to work with him as a partner. Baum was co-author of the Baum-Welch algorithm – something that would go on to become a big part of Monemetrics. It worked by predicting outcomes from a series of events, without knowing the underlying parameters or variables. These unpredictable series of events are called hidden Markov chains.

Baum-Welch's algorithm worked by making educated guesses – analyzing a chain of events and estimating probabilities. For example, without knowing the rules of baseball, it could estimate what would happen next by simply analyzing patterns in the play. It would go on to be enormously important for the future, in speech-recognition technology and even for Google's search engine.

Simons and Baum figured that a predictive model like this would be very useful for monitoring movements in the markets. This was 1979, before the days of digitized trading, so to measure data, they stuck lots of graphs and charts over the walls of their HQ – a little office in a Long Island strip-mall.

Trading only in currencies at first, they began to make lots of money. In one memorable episode, Baum was relaxing on the beach when epiphany struck. He realized that they must buy lots of British pounds. Margaret Thatcher, the new British prime minister was keeping the pound unnaturally low. From Baum's estimations, it would rise very soon, so he rushed from the beach straight into the Long Island office and harangued Simons to buy while it was still low. Suddenly, as he predicted, the pound began to climb rapidly.

And like the sea rushing into a hollow, Monemetric's fund grew by tens of millions of dollars.

SIMONS NAMED HIS MONEMETRICS FUND AFTER A CHARACTER IN A JOSEPH CONRAD NOVEL – AND THIS WAS REVEALING.

Monemetrics was Simons' first real venture into the world of finance. He began assembling a team of mathematicians around him and Baum, including old friends from college. After he'd convinced others to join him in this endeavor, he set up a hedge fund, where they'd manage their investments.

He named it "Nimroy." This was an anagram of the Joseph Conrad novel Lord Jim and the Royal Bank of Bermuda, which handled the company's money transfers for tax purposes (namely, avoiding them).

The name blended high finance with a character who wrestles with ideals of honor and morality. In Lord Jim a promising young seaman panics and abandons a sinking ship, leaving its passengers to the mercy of the waves. The rest of the book follows the story of the disgraced seaman, as he wrestles with his conscience and past.

According to a young hire at Monemetrics, Greg Hullender, Simons associated himself with the seaman in Conrad's novel. As Jim had jettisoned his more "noble" career as an academic for the lure of enormous riches, the seaman's moral struggle resonated. Abandoning a ship was a terrible black mark against a seaman's honor, and Jim had begun to think that he'd done something similar by getting into the world of finance.

Just as in Conrad's novel, there would be troubled waters for Monemetrics in its early stages. Though they were buying low, they weren't selling high. In one instance they had bought into gold, and gold had skyrocketed to $865 an ounce. Monemetrics didn't sell quickly enough and gold crashed very shortly afterwards to $500 an ounce. They began to incur more and more losses like this, reaching a point where the fund was losing millions of dollars daily.

Then one day, Greg Hullender walked into Simons' office and found him lying down on the couch. Hullender inquired if he was OK. Jim, supine, began to reveal his doubts: he wondered if he simply didn't know what he was doing. He brought up Lord Jim again, remarking that the character was someone with a high opinion of himself, but had failed miserably. He added, darkly, "He had a really good death, though."

SIMONS INTRODUCED COMPUTERS INTO THE WORLD OF INVESTMENT WITH GREAT SUCCESS.

Fortunately, the early losses that Monemetrics incurred would soon be overturned. But first, they had to develop a far more accurate system to read movements in the markets.

While other investors were relying on old-fashioned intuition and business news for their predictions, Simons decided that he would feed data through computers – a technology that was thin on the ground in the early 1980s. Renaming Monemetrics "Renaissance Technologies," he looked ahead onto a brave new world of investing.

He started by collecting great amounts of historical data and feeding it directly into his computer. Simons bought stacks of books from the World Bank, reels of magnetic tape from commodity exchanges, and records of currency prices going back to before World War II.

He did this so that he could analyze old market movements for consistent patterns that might apply to the present. However, the present was increasingly volatile. Though there were broad resemblances, it was very difficult to extrapolate patterns that would be relevant to the present from this historical data. So, the goal had to be monitoring the present as swiftly as possible.

To do this they bought lots of expensive computers, enormous amounts of data storage, and high-speed connections to market data. This provided live market prices that no-one else in the investment world had access to.

They combined this flood of data with Baum's predictive mathematics, improved by another of the team Simons had assembled, prize-winning algebraist James Ax. Refining Baum's method so that it would be better able to predict more "dynamic" series, like the wildly fluctuating markets of the 1980s, Ax's tweaks improved their returns. Also, by the time they'd refined their model, more powerful computers became available, improving their capacity to monitor new data.

After this point, Simons and Ax named the Renaissance hedge fund "Medallion" to reflect the mathematics successes they'd both had in earlier times. And leveraging their combined brainpower, the Medallion fund became Renaissance's most profitable portfolio.

Later, it would become famed for having the best record in investing history, returning more than 66 percent in annual returns and trading profits of more than $100 billion. They hadn't "solved" the markets, but they'd found a way to trace their subtlest tremors and shifts.

SIMONS' CAREER BROUGHT HIM INTO THE AMBIT OF A BRILLIANT MAN WHO WOULD GO ON TO COURT GREAT CONTROVERSY.

As Renaissance expanded its investment activities it searched for more brainpower. One of these new recruits was a man named Robert Mercer, who'd been working for the computer giant IBM. He'd had great success at IBM, laying the groundwork for advances in speech-recognition technology.

A brilliant coder, he was exactly the kind of person that Renaissance were looking for. Mercer had spent his childhood and adolescence at a computer keyboard – or at least as much as he could during the 1960s and 70s. As a young man, he'd been particularly inspired by a meeting with Neil Armstrong, who'd come to give a talk to budding computer scientists at a youth science camp in the mountains of West Virginia.

After graduating from college, Mercer had gone on to work in a weapons laboratory as a computer programmer. There, after making some striking improvements to the speed of lab computers, he was told by his bosses, who had little interest in his achievements, not to bother anyone. According to Mercer, they were more interested in successfully checking boxes as they consumed the government's research budget. This turned Mercer into an opponent of government. Later he would take the view that individuals need to be self-sufficient and avoid state aid.

At Renaissance, his talent for coding helped to identify flaws and glitches in the system, boosting the firm's great success throughout the 1990s. But it was his political affiliations that would go on to define him.

Quiet and with a laconic sense of humor, he didn't immediately appear the sort to have deep ideological convictions. But he did, and they led him to fund right-wing political movements and publications, including the website Breitbart, and, later, the campaign to elect Donald Trump as US president.

This contrasted with Jim Simons, who was a Democrat, donating millions to their campaigns over the years. While working together in the cut and thrust of finance, these differences weren't all that pressing. But later, when Mercer financed Donald Trump's run at the presidency in 2016, he was forced to step down from his position at Renaissance – a co-CEO by that point – after a furious backlash from investors. Jim Simons is thought to have made the final call.

Simons and Mercer – two idiosyncratic geniuses, one in math, the other in computing. The pair would go on to have an enormous impact on the world in their different ways, disrupting lives for better and for worse, as they quietly tapped at their keyboards.

WHEN ALL IS SAID AND DONE, JIM SIMONS' CV IS AN ASTONISHING DOCUMENT.

The Medicis were a powerful banking family who determined the course of politics, art, and royal power in medieval Italy and beyond. It might be said, not without accuracy, that Jim Simons is something like a modern-day equivalent of a member of that dynasty. His achievements, when all is totted-up, are truly awe-inspiring.

First off, he's the most successful trader in the history of modern finance.

No one in the investment world even comes close to his profits at Renaissance. Those trading legends, like Warren Buffett, George Soros, Peter Lynch, Steve Cohen, and Ray Dalio all fall short. As noted earlier, the Medallion fund's total profits are calculated to be around £100 billion. And still, in recent years, Renaissance has been hitting $7 billion annually in trading gains. That's more than the yearly revenue of giant brand-names, including Levi Strauss, Hyatt Hotels, and Hasbro. Today, Simons is worth around $23 billion, making him wealthier than Elon Musk, Rupert Murdoch, and Laurene Powell Jobs – Steve Jobs's widow.

And the pioneering trading methods that Renaissance used went on to shape fields far beyond the world of finance.

Indeed, they've been embraced by almost every industry. Take the mass statistic crunching that Renaissance and Monemetrics did – there is no professional sports team in the world that doesn't do the same now. Then there's turning tasks over to machines – think of the military's growing reliance on robots, or health professionals using computers to diagnose illnesses. Or the use of algorithms in pretty much every area where forecasting is required.

But Simons' influence doesn't stop at industry. Later on, after he had managed to make lots and lots of money, he became a great benefactor.

Just like the Medicis, who were patrons of great Renaissance painters and scholars, Simons has subsidized organizations and individuals all around the globe. To list just a few of them: he established the Simons Foundation for education and health, founded the Math for America initiative, aided the development of Nepalese healthcare, and donated great sums to Stony Brook University.

Today, Simons is notoriously difficult to contact. Current and former employees are sworn to secrecy regarding Renaissance's trading secrets.

From a boy that liked to close his eyes and dream of numbers, Jim Simons has come to be one of the most powerful and enigmatic people in the world.

FINAL SUMMARY:

The key message in this book:

After a successful early career as a gifted mathematician, Jim Simons went on to crack Soviet codes, before revolutionizing the world of investment with Renaissance Technologies. Through the use of mass data, algorithms, and computing, he changed the way global finance works. After amassing great wealth, he now acts as a powerful benefactor to a vast array of organizations and progressive initiatives.

ABOUT CTPrint

CTPrint is dedicated to creating high-quality summaries of non-fiction books to help you through the bestseller list each week!

We cover books in self-help, business, personal development, science & technology, health & fitness, history, and memoir/biography. Our books are expertly written and professionally edited to provide top-notch content. We're here to help you decide which books to invest your time and money reading.

Absorb everything you need to know in 20 minutes or less!

We release new summaries each and every week, so join our mailing list to stay up-to-date and get free summaries right in your inbox!

Made in the USA
San Bernardino, CA
17 December 2019